2005 | Higher

[BLANK PAGE]

Pocket answer section for SQA Higher German 2005–2008

Published by Leckie & Leckie Ltd, 3rd Floor, 4 Queen Street, Edinburgh EH2 1JE
tel: 0131 220 6831, fax: 0131 225 9987, enquiries@leckieandleckie.co.uk, www.leckieandleckie.co.uk

Higher German
Reading and Directed Writing
2005

SECTION I – READING

1. *Any two of:*
    - she feels like a star/celebrity
      she feels as if the red carpet has been rolled out for her
      she feels as if the red carpet is going to be rolled out for her
    - her eyes (start to) shine/light up/sparkle/gleam/glisten/glitter/glint
      her eyes become bright
    - her heart beats/pumps/goes fast**er**
      her heart rate increases
      her heart races
    - she has/gets butterflies in her stomach/tummy/belly
      she gets butterflies

2. *Any two of:*
    - she wants clothes like the pop singers she sees on TV
      she wants to look like the pop singers she sees on TV
      she sees pop singers on TV in their cool clothes and goes out to buy clothes like that/those clothes
    - a **voice in her head** tells her to buy things/shop
      a **voice in her head** is egging her on
    - she **wants** to be/look attractive/beautiful/pretty/popular/ loved

3. they made fun of/mocked her
    they joked and bitched about her
    they made jokes/nasty/snide remarks about her
    they made jokes etc. about her masses of shopping bags
    or
    she withdrew/drifted away from them
    she pulled back from them
    she drew/stood back/moved away from them
    she became isolated/detached from them
    she is no longer in that group

4. *Any three of:*
    - she got **money** from her grandparents/grandma/grandpa
    - she borrowed/got a loan of money
      she was lent money/she asked for a loan/she got a loan
    - she **asked her family** for money at Christmas/birthdays
      she would wish for money from her parents at …
      she wanted money from her parents at …

4. continued
    - she took money from her savings account
      she began to spend money from her savings account
      she started eating into her savings
      she raided/ate into her savings
      she stole from her account

5. (*a*) the more she had/earned, the more she spent/bought/went shopping
        since/as she had more, she spent more
        she spent/shopped even more
        her spending really took off

    (*b*) they thought it was good that she was learning to handle/deal with money/budget
        they wanted her to learn to handle/manage money
        to let her learn how to handle money
        they wanted her to learn her way round money
        they wanted her to learn how to use money properly
        they wanted her to learn money management
        they wanted her to learn responsibility with money
        their daughter had to learn to handle money

6. (*a*) (sometimes) she did not know/had no idea/sense of how much she **had spent**

    (*b*)
        - they depressed her/she was/felt/became depressed
          they weighed her down/troubled her deeply/more and more
        - she suffered/spent sleepless nights
          she lost sleep at night/could not sleep (at night)
          she had trouble sleeping
        - she couldn't see herself living a normal life
          she saw herself without the/any possibility/opportunity of a normal life
          she saw herself with/she worried about the possibility of not leading a normal life
          she wondered if she could/will lead a normal life
          if she stays like this, she will be without the possibility of leading a normal life

Higher German
Reading and Directed Writing
2005 (cont.)

7. (a) she banned herself from going to town/stayed away from the town/imposed a city ban on herself/prescribed herself a town ban or went out without any money/took no money with her when she went out (both elements required)

  (b) window-shopping **and** made lists of/wrote down things to buy
  or
  made lists of/wrote down things to buy **and** when she had money
  She would go window-shopping and make a list of all the things she wanted to buy
  She wrote lists of the things she wanted to buy when/if/as soon as she had money (again)/so she could come back when she had money/with the money

8. *Any two of:*
   - she burst/broke into tears/was crying a lot/was frequently tearful/would start to cry
   - she was nervous/jittery/edgy/**looking** anxious
   - she began to/would shake/tremble/shake/quiver/ got the shakes/she was caught trembling
   - she couldn't concentrate/lacked/lost concentration

9. - she does not borrow (money)
     she has stopped borrowing money
     she does not get her friends to lend her money any more
     she does not get loans from her friends
   - she has paid back almost/nearly/practically everything/most of it
     she has paid back most of what she borrowed/owes
     she has paid back most of her debts
     she has paid almost all of them back
     she has returned nearly everything

10. My parents told me that I should go to the doctor. And that was the best thing that could have happened to me. The doctor spent a long time talking to me. For the first time I spoke quite openly about my shopping addiction.

SECTION II – DIRECTED WRITING

Please refer to **2008 German Reading and Directed Writing** Section II – Directed/Writing. The table on pages 11-12 details what is required to produce a good essay answer.

Higher German
Listening/Writing
2005

SECTION A

1. (a) • trains/training twice
   - one or two games/matches etc.
   - he plays once or twice
   - game/match once or twice

  (b) • once a fortnight/every fortnight
   - once every two weeks
   - every second week(end)/fortnight/two weeks
   - every other weekend
   - every two weekends
   - twice a month

2. *Any two of:*
   - boys' appearance matters to girls
     girls think it is important how boys look
     girls like boys who look good
   - To gain a point here, candidates must refer clearly to boys **looking** fit/sporty etc.
     girls like a boy with a sporty physique/figure/shape
     girls like boys who look fit/are in good shape
     girls like boys with an athletic/muscular figure
     girls like fit guys because they have a nicer/better body
     girls are attracted to a sporty figure
   - girls find a fat boyfriend embarrassing
     fat/fatter people are unattractive
     girls don't want a fat boyfriend
     girls don't like fat guys

3. *Any two of:*
   - watches sports programmes on TV
     watches sport on TV
     watches (favourite) sport (programme) on Saturdays
   - reads sports magazines
   - plays table-tennis – **with his brother**
     plays table-tennis **when he has time**

4. (a) going to go out/away **more** (often)
     (hopes) to go out **more** (often)
     allowed out **more** (often)

  (b) at a dance/dance-hall/club/disco
     dancing/clubbing
     or
     in/at an ice-cream parlour/at an (ice-)café

5. he is the (only) goalkeeper
   or
   he has a responsibility/duty towards the team/the others
   he does not want to let the team down
   he owes it to the team/he has to be there for his team
   he is committed to his team
   he is answerable to his team
   or
   his girlfriend/she would/should/will understand
   he would expect girlfriend to understand
   girlfriend will be understanding

6. (a)
- he would miss/cancel/drop/skive off training.
  he would miss a training session
  he would cut back on his training
- once a fortnight
  every two/second/other weeks

(b) cut back on her hobby/one of her interests
do something similar/the same for him
give up something she does/a hobby (for him)
give up something as well
sacrifice her hobby/hobbies
make sacrifices (for him)
compromise on her hobbies

7.
- she/they will/would understand if he does not have time (at weekend)
  understanding if/when he has no time (at weekend)
  she would understand at weekends
  more understanding why he has to go to training
  they would understand if he was too busy
  they would understand his sporting commitments
- she might come to the odd game
  she might come to a match from time to time
  she might come and watch him play
  she could support his team

8.
- not/no more than twice a week
  maximum of twice a week
- Saturday **evening/night**

9. (a) each/every day/daily/on a daily basis

(b)
- they forget (about) everything else
  they forget everything around them
  they forget about things/the world around them
  they forget everything apart from each other
- should not abandon/drop/forget friends/team **because of a girl/ relationship/and only focus on the girlfriend/just to spend time with a girlfriend/and let your relationship take over your life/over a girl**
  love life should not interfere with your sport
  girlfriends are not as important as the team

SECTION B

Please refer to **2008 German Listening/Writing** Section B. The table on pages 14-15 details what is required to produce a good essay answer.

Higher German
Reading and Directed Writing
2006

An underlining indicates that a particular word or idea must be present in the answer for the answer to be acceptable eg <u>Friend's</u> <u>birthday</u> (party) – separate underlinings of "Friend's" and "birthday" indicate that the candidate must show understanding not only that this was a <u>birthday</u> party, but that the party was for a <u>friend</u>.

By similar token, a phrase such as "<u>from all over Europe</u>" should be underlined as a phrase (and not as single words, ie "<u>from</u> <u>all</u> <u>over</u> <u>Europe</u>"), as it is the phrase and not the individual words which are important.

SECTION I – READING

1. *Any two of:*

- their life is expensive
  being a student/a young person is expensive
  they need money for: 2 of their phone, clothes, the cinema, holidays
- pocket money (usually) not enough
  pocket money does not cover their costs
  the money they get from their parents is not enough/insufficient/inadequate
- so that they do not have to rely on parents
  so that they can earn their own money
  so that they do not need to go to their parents
  it is a welcome alternative to the parental purse
  to stop taking money from their parent's purse/pocket

2. (*a*)
- delivers/distributes <u>TV (guides) and other magazines/illustrated papers</u>
  OR delivers magazines/papers/does a paper-round <u>twice a week</u>
  OR delivers/distributes magazines/papers/does a paper-round <u>on his bike</u>

(*b*)
- <u>exchange</u>/<u>school</u>-trip to France <u>and</u> trip/journey/holiday/travel to Scotland

(*c*)
- mother saw/read advert in the paper
  mother found the job/it in the paper
  mother showed him the ad in the paper
  his mum read about it in the newspaper

3. (*a*)
- divides his round into 3
  divides the area into 3 rounds
  does it in 3 trips
  he shares it between 3 tours
  in 3 tours of the district
- does one round after the other (on his bike)
  does each in turn

3. (*b*)
- has to go out in all weathers/no matter the weather/he has to work in any weather conditions
  customers want their magazines in all weathers/despite the weather
  OR
- it is awful/difficult/bad/not good/rubbish/silly/stupid/a pain when it is hot/there is (black) ice
  it seems stupid when it is hot/there is (black) ice

(*c*) *Any two of:*
- easy money
- fun/likes doing it/enjoys his job
- does not interfere with his school work/school work does not suffer/school work can fit around it

4. (*a*)
- financial ~~independence~~/freedom
  she was financially dependent/she is financially independent

(*b*)
- because of the hourly rate/pay/wages <u>and</u> tips
  good pay <u>and</u> tips

5. *Any two of:*
- every customer/guest is different/the work is varied
- she finds working/dealing/getting on with people easy/the contact with people is easy for her
  she finds it easy to relate to people
- you learn to approach people in a relaxed way
  you learn to be relaxed with/around/towards people
  you learn to be cool with people
- (you learn) to be friendly/nice/pleasant towards unfriendly/unkind people/guests/customers/clients
- some days/sometimes/at times/there are days when it is/can be stressful/can cause a lot of stress

6. (*a*)
- because of her school leaving/end of school/final exams
  so her work doesn't affect her marks/grades/results/exams
  she does not want her school grades affected
  so she does not spoil her school grades
  so that work does not impair/get in the way of her school grades
  she has to concentrate on her grades
  to get the grades she wants
  to get her grades

6. (*b*)
- she's improved her mental arithmetic
  she is better at mental arithmetic/sums in her head/working things out in her head/counting in her head/calculating in her head
  with mental arithmetic

7. (*a*) *Any two of:*
- direct contact with the public/customers
- fills/stacks the shelves/fills the empty shelves
- in charge of/responsible for the empties in the drinks department

(*b*) *Any two of:*
- it's good/nice he is earning money
  they are pleased he is earning money
- his brother did same job before/once/earlier
  his brother had the/this/that job
- there have been no problems with school
  it did not affect his/their schooling
  the job gave his brother no problems with school

8. *Any one of:*
- you have a different/new attitude towards money
  you have a different feel(ing) for money
  you feel differently about money
  you have another feeling for money
  you get a new feeling for money
  you get a better understanding of money
  you get a better sense about money
  you get a different outlook on money
  it has given him an appreciation of the value of money
- you think about/consider how you spend your money/what you spend it on/what you buy with it
  you spend it in a more considered way
  you are more careful with money/you take more care with money
- he would not want to do this for ever/life
  he would not want to do this job all his life/his whole life

9. „Ich weiß genau, wo man alles im Supermarkt finden kann
I know exactly/precisely/the exact place where you can find/one/people can find everything in the supermarket/all the things in the supermarket/anything in the supermarket/where everything can be found in the supermarket

und welche Flaschen wir zurücknehmen dürfen", sagt Andreas.
and which/what bottles we are allowed/permitted to/may take back/accept says/said Andreas

9. (continued)

Wenn Kunden genervt und unfreundlich sind,
If/When/Whenever customers/clients are irritated/worked up/annoyed/stressed and unfriendly/unpleasant

hat er seine eigene Taktik entwickelt:
he has developed/he has worked out/he has devised/his own strategy/strategies/tactics/tactic

„Man muss sympathisch sein und den Kunden helfen."
You/One must be/have to be/need to be pleasant/nice/congenial and help the customers/clients/be helpful to the customers/provide help for the customers.

SECTION II – DIRECTED WRITING

Please refer to **2008 German Reading and Directed Writing** Section II – Directed/Writing. The table on pages 11-12 details what is required to produce a good essay answer.

Higher German
Listening/Writing
2006

SECTION A

1. • so that they are healthy/healthier/fit when they
   are older/old/adults/in later life/in the future
   so that they aren't unhealthy when they are
   older

2. *Any two of:*
   • goes jogging/running with friend(s)
     OR goes jogging/running regularly
   • gets/goes to/takes badminton lessons
   • plays volleyball twice a week

3. • would/does not go to McDonalds/fast food
     restaurants every day/daily
     does not go to McDonalds much/regularly/very
     often
     does not eat fast food every day
     rarely/seldom eats fast food/McDonalds
     does not eat much/a lot of fast food
     would/does not live off fast food
     avoids/keeps clear of fast food
     eats a limited amount of fast food
   • eats a lot/plenty of salad and vegetables

4. • few(er)/not (as/so) many/less/not a lot of
     Germans go to fast food restaurants
   • Scotland/Britain/here – (lots of) families with
     young/small/little children eat/live on fast
     food/go there
     young families go there

5. • (a lot of) fruit each/every day/daily
   • not too/so many/much/not a lot of
     sweets/sweeties/candy/confectionery

6. • sometimes + at the weekend
     now and again/then + at the weekend
     from time to time + at the weekend
     occasionally + at the weekend
     not very often + at the weekend
     not regularly + at the weekend
     every so often + at the weekend
     some weekends

7. (a) • there is a problem in cities/big(ger)
         towns/in the city
         no more or less than in Scotland
         it is much the same as in Scotland
         no better or worse than in Scotland
         it is pretty much equal to Scotland
         not any great difference between Scotland
         and Germany

   (b) • can drink/buy beer or wine at 16 (in pub)
       • can buy it in shop at 16

8. *Any two from:*
   • it is unhealthy/bad for your health
     it is bad for you
   • she does not smoke/never has smoked (and
     never will)
   • (lots of) young people/teenagers do it because
     it is/looks cool
     young people do it to look cool
   • people smoke due to peer pressure

9. • a lot of/(too) many people are too fat
     a lot of people have health problems because of
     weight/they are fat
   • little/small/young children who are
     very/really/too fat/really overweight/obese
     there are (some) very fat small children
     some small children are very fat
     little/small/young children who cannot/are
     unable to do sport because of their size/because
     they are so fat

10. *Any three of:*
    • German children/they eat a sandwich/bread
      (and butter)/roll/apple at the interval/at break
      Germans take a sandwich to school
    • sweets not sold in schools (in Germany)
      you cannot buy sweets in schools
    • Scots eat crisps at break time/at school
      In Scotland they eat crisps at break time/at
      school
      Germans do not eat crisps at school
    • (German) children do sport in the
      afternoon/after school/after lunch
      almost every German child does sport
      lots of sports clubs for them

SECTION B

Please refer to **2008 German Listening/
Writing** Section B. The table on pages 14-15
details what is required to produce a good essay
answer.

Higher German
Reading and Directed Writing
2007

SECTION I—READING

1. (a) He worked on a farm in Australia (in 2001)

(b) *Any two of*
- It is cramped/limited/crowded/packed/ enclosed/not open enough/restricting/ constricting/claustrophobic/limiting he feels confined and closed in/it feels too small
- too much stress/too stressful
- too much pressure to succeed/achieve/ perform/work hard/do well

(c) when the children are older/grown-up/adults when the children grow up

2. (a)
- <u>with her qualifications</u> she has/will have.... .. good prospects/opportunities/chances in Australia... a good chance of succeeding/ doing well/getting a job in Australia... a good/greater/better chance in Australia Her qualifications as a nurse could be wanted in Australia
- her daughter can/could start school at (age of) four in a year her daughter will be able to start school in Australia

(b) she does not have the money/the 2000 dollars.... ....for a visa and the test she'd have to sit the cost/expense of the visa and test she would have to sit

3. *Any two of*
- it/you can/could/might be lonely it is sometimes lonely
- (when you are) sitting <u>quietly/silently</u> in a corner
- you cannot understand <u>jokes</u>/one <u>joke</u> in English
- to speak to Australians you need to know/learn about Australian/their politics/sport/humour

4. (a) high cost <u>and</u> time needed to return to Germany it costs/takes a lot of time and money to go/get back to Germany/to visit Germany it costs/takes a lot of time and money to come (back) from Australia

(b) *Any three of*
- <u>often</u> works six days a week
- has never worked so hard/so long/such long hours in his life
- no lunch/dinner/midday break even in 40 degree heat
- pay/wages/money/salary is less <u>than in Germany/at home</u> wages are low compared with Germany

5. (a)
- the smell of smoke/it smells of smoke
- the laugh/call/cry of the kookaburra/a bird

(b) met and married Marcel/met her husband/ met someone and got married

(c) their openness/they are (very) open it is easy to get to know them/make contact with them/you make acquaintances quickly/you make/form contacts quickly

6. (a) the school system is not so/very good good schools are generally/mostly/usually/normally/ mainly/(very) often/predominantly/as a rule private and expensive

(b)
- she wants her children to go to school in Germany/a German school
- Antje will/wants to take over/take on/run her parents' business/firm/company in Berlin

7. „Gerhard Scheller hat seinen deutschen Pass abgegeben"
Gerhard Scheller has given up/in/back gave up/in/back has handed in/over/back handed in/over/back his German passport

„und ist jetzt stolz darauf, australischer Staatsbürger zu sein."
and is now proud of/about being to be an Australian citizen/national

„Gerhard und seine Frau Britta haben sich kennen gelernt"
Gerhard and his wife Britta met got to know each/one other came to know each other

„als sie in Hamburg Informatik studierten."
when/whilst they studied/did they were studying/doing computing science/computer science/IT/Information Technology/Information Systems/Information Science in Hamburg.

„Seit 1994 leben sie in einem Vorort von Sydney."
Since 1994 they have been living/they have lived in a suburb of Sydney/Sydney suburb.

SECTION II – DIRECTED WRITING

Please refer to **2008 German Reading and Directed Writing** Section II – Directed/Writing. The table on pages 11-12 details what is required to produce a good essay answer.

Higher German Listening/Writing 2007

Section A

1. *Any two of*
   - a lot/lots/(so) much/loads/a huge amount to learn/study/do/revise
     she had so much work to do for them
   - a lot of/lots of/loads of/(so) many books to read
   - essays to write

2. (*a*)
   - She had a revision/study/learning plan/programme
     She made a timetable for learning/a revision timetable
     OR
   - She studied/learned new/different things/stuff/topics each week
     She studied something else/new things each week

   (*b*) *Any two of*
   - She did not have any (free time)/She had none.
     No (more) free time.
     It took away her free time
     Her time was all taken up
   - Could not see/meet/go out with her friends as/so often/ as/so much
   - Hardly any time for sport
     Practically/almost no time for sport
     She did hardly any sport

3. • She was pleased/happy/satisfied/content with her mark(s)/ grade(s)/result(s)
      She thought she had done very well.
      OR
   • she got (an average of) 1.5

4. • 3 to 4 days/3 or 4 days of parties/partying
      They had a party/partied for 3 or 4 days/3 to 4 days
      There was a 3-4 day party
   • (People from) school organised/had/held/threw/arranged (big)"do"/event/party/celebration/dance/ceremony

5. (*a*) a big/large group/crowd/clique of friends/pals
       (about) 10 friends/pals
       10 of her friends/pals

   (*b*) *Any two of*
   - the flight(s)/plane(s)
     the plane journey/ticket(s)
   - accommodation/somewhere to stay
     where to spend the night
   - activities
     what (they were going) to do
     everything/things to do

5. (*c*) • internet/websites and travel agent/bureau/office
        • booked it on-line and got info from the travel agent

6. *Any three of*
   - three of the group could not go/make it
     three people pulled out
   - one – could not go because of parents
     one – because of her parents/because her parents banned her
     Corinna's parents would not let her go
     Corinna was not allowed to go
   - one – could not go because of work
     Mario found/got a job/had to work
   - one – could not go because of illness
     Nadine took ill

7. *Any three from*
   - went out a lot
   - relaxing by the sea/on the beach/relaxing in the sun/by the sea in the sun (Answer must have 2 elements of relax+sea+sun.)
   - spent a week doing nothing (at all)
   - went on a couple/few/some excursions/(day)trips/outings
   - did some sightseeing/saw the sights/went to see the sights

8. • Last chance/opportunity/time to spend time with/to be with/to see your friends
   • before going to university or starting a job
      before university or work/job.

SECTION B

Please refer to **2008 German Listening/Writing** Section B. The table on pages 14-15 details what is required to produce a good essay answer.

Higher German
Reading and Directed Writing
2008

SECTION I – READING

1. • study/studies/college/university or
   apprenticeship/train(ing)/further
   education/become a trainee/learn a trade <u>and</u> (if
   study) what (to study)
   • stay at home or move out/take off/leave (your
   house/home)/go elsewhere <u>and</u> (if move out),
   where (to)

2. (a) it was the best decision ever/so far/yet
   it was the best decision she ever made

   (b) *Any two from:*
   • she has met/got to know
     wonderful/great/marvellous people
   • she has experienced (so)
     many/countless/numerous/a large number
     of/a lot of new things
     she has had so many new experiences
   • she has become/she is (now) <u>much more</u>
     independent/<u>really</u> independent
   • she has brought/taken/got her English up
     to a high/advanced level/standard

3. (a) *Any two from:*
   • attend/go to college
   • voluntary/charity work
   • language class/course

   (b) a first-aid course <u>and</u> a Spanish course

4. (a) meets friends in cafés, to watch videos/films/for
   a video/film evening/movie-night or in a
   karaoke bar

   (b) it only takes (about) an hour/it takes (just)
   under an hour in the train to get to New
   York/Manhattan (from where she stays/New
   Jersey)

5. (a) *Any three from:*
   • <u>family</u> with <u>two</u> hyperactive children
     some <u>families</u> have <u>2</u> hyperactive children
   • unfriendly granny lives in the house
     granny who hates young people lives in the
     house
   • <u>have to/must</u> work until 10.00 pm/22.00
     <u>every night</u>
   • only allowed to eat certain
     things/particular food from the fridge
     not allowed particular things to eat from
     the fridge

   (b) tiny/small/little room under the stairs

6. (a) they wanted as little as possible to do with their
   child(ren)

   (b) give the 8 year old (boy/son) 70 tablets and/then
   take the boy/child to the psychiatrist

7. *Any two from:*
   • not allowed out during the week/on week-days
     cannot go out during the week/on week-days
     are banned from going out during the week/on
     week-days
     have a going out ban during the week/on week-
     days
   • (must) be in/home at/before/by 10.00 pm/22.00
     have a curfew to be in at 10
     have a 10 pm curfew
   • can stay out/away all night as long as they are
     back/in/home (in time) to waken children
     can stay out all night as long as they wake up
     the children

8. *Any one from:*
   • be as honest/genuine/truthful as possible
   • think carefully/exactly about what you/to
     want/expect from the year
     consider what you want from the year
   • ask all your questions during the telephone
     interview
     use a/the telephone interview as an opportunity
     to put questions to the family
     use the telephone interview and ask questions
     have a telephone interview and ask about things

9. *Any two from:*
   • if that is your attitude/in this mind set/in that
     case/if you do/(because) then hardly anything
     can go wrong
   • you can <u>look forward</u> to a great/brilliant/
     fantastic/super/mad year
   • new experiences are guaranteed - positive/good
     as well as/and/or negative/bad

10. „In meiner Familie bin ich für zwei Schulkinder
    verantwortlich."
    In my family
    I am
    responsible for/in charge of
    two
    school-children/school-kids/children of school age

    „Daher habe ich jeden Morgen frei."
    Because of this/that/For this/that reason/So/That's
    why/Therefore/Hence/This/That means/Due to that
    I have
    every morning/the morning/(the) mornings/in the
    morning(s)
    off./free.
    That's why I am off/free every morning.

    „Am Nachmittag bin ich hauptsächlich dazu da,"
    In the afternoon(s)
    I am
    mainly/chiefly
    here/there
    In the afternoon the main reason I am there is

Higher German
Reading and Directed Writing
2008 (cont.)

10. continued

„die Kinder zur richtigen Zeit an den richtigen
Ort zu bringen"
to bring/of bringing/(I) bring/to take/of taking/(I)
take/to get/of getting/(I) get
the children

to the right/correct/proper place
at the right/correct/proper time

„und ihnen am Abend etwas zu kochen".
and
(to) cook/cooking/(I) cook
something for them/them something (to eat)
in the evening(s).

SECTION II – DIRECTED WRITING

INSERT TABLES FROM 2007 DIRECTED WRITING

SECTION II—DIRECTED WRITING

Category	Mark	Content	Accuracy	Language Resource – Variety, Range, Structures
Very Good	15	• All bullet points are covered fully, in a balanced way, including a number of complex sentences. • Some candidates may also provide additional information. • A wide range of verbs/verb forms, tenses and constructions is used. • Overall this comes over as a competent, well thought-out account of the event which reads naturally.	• The candidate handles all aspects of grammar and spelling accurately, although the language may contain some minor errors or even one more serious error. • Where the candidate attempts to use language more appropriate to post-Higher, a slightly higher number of inaccuracies need not detract from the overall very good impression.	• The candidate is comfortable with almost all the grammar used and generally uses a different verb or verb form in each sentence. • There is good use of a variety of tenses, adjectives, adverbs and prepositional phrases and, where appropriate, word order. • The candidate uses co-ordinating conjunctions and subordinate clauses throughout the writing. • The language flows well.
Good	12	• All bullet points are addressed, generally quite fully, and some complex sentences may be included. • The response to one bullet point may be thin, although other bullet points are dealt with in some detail. • The candidate uses a reasonable range of verbs/verb forms and other constructions.	• The candidate generally handles verbs and other parts of speech accurately but simply. • There may be some errors in spelling, adjective endings and, where relevant, case endings. • Use of accents may be less secure. • Where the candidate is attempting to use more complex vocabulary and structures, these may be less successful, although basic structures are used accurately. • There may be minor misuse of dictionary.	• There may be less variety in the verbs used. • The candidate is able to use a significant amount of complex sentences. • In one bullet point the language may be more basic than might otherwise be expected at this level. • Overall the writing will be competent, mainly correct, but pedestrian.
Satisfactory	9	• The candidate uses mainly simple, more basic sentences. • The language is perhaps repetitive and uses a limited range of verbs and fixed phrases not appropriate to this level. • In some examples, one or two bullet points may be less fully addressed. • In some cases, the content may be similar to that of good or very good examples, but with some serious accuracy issues.	• The verbs are generally correct, but basic. • Tenses may be inconsistent, with present tenses being used at times instead of past tenses. • There are quite a few errors in other parts of speech – personal pronouns, gender of nouns, adjective endings, cases, singular/plural confusion – and in the use of accents. • Some prepositions may be inaccurate or omitted e.g. I went the town. • While the language may be reasonably accurate in three or four bullet points, in the remaining two control of the language structure may deteriorate significantly. • Overall, there is more correct than incorrect.	• The candidate copes with the past tense of some verbs. • A limited range of verbs is used to address some of the bullet points. • Candidate relies on a limited range of vocabulary and structures. • Occasionally, the past participle is incorrect or the auxiliary verb is omitted. • Sentences may be basic and mainly brief. • There is minimal use of adjectives, probably mainly after "is" e.g. The boss was helpful. • The candidate has a weak knowledge of plurals. • There may be several spelling errors e.g. reversal of vowel combinations.

Category	Mark	Content	Accuracy	Language Resource – Variety, Range, Structures
Unsatisfactory	6	• In some cases the content may be basic. • In other cases there may be little difference in content between Satisfactory and Unsatisfactory. • The language is repetitive, with undue reliance on fixed phrases and a limited range of common basic verbs such as *to be, to have, to play, to watch*. • While the language used to address the more predictable bullet points may be accurate, serious errors occur when the candidate attempts to address the less predictable areas. • The Directed Writing may be presented as a single paragraph.	• Ability to form tenses is inconsistent. • In the use of the perfect tense the auxiliary verb is omitted on a number of occasions. • There may be confusion between the singular and plural form of verbs. • There are errors in many other parts of speech – gender of nouns, cases, singular/plural confusion, spelling and, where appropriate, word order. • Several errors are serious, perhaps showing mother tongue interference. • There may be one sentence which is not intelligible to a sympathetic native speaker. • One area may be very weak. • Overall, there is more incorrect than correct.	• The candidate copes mainly only with the predictable language required at the earlier bullet points. • The verbs "was" and "went" may also be used correctly. • There is inconsistency in the use of various expressions, especially verbs. • Sentences are more basic. • An English word may appear in the writing or a word may be omitted. • There may be an example of serious dictionary misuse.
Poor	3	• The content and language may be very basic. • However, in many cases the content may be little different from that expected at Unsatisfactory or even at Satisfactory.	• Many of the verbs are incorrect or even omitted. • There are many errors in other parts of speech – personal pronouns, gender of nouns, adjective endings, cases, singular/plural confusion, word order, spelling. • Prepositions are not used correctly. • The language is probably inaccurate throughout the writing. • Some sentences may not be understood by a sympathetic native speaker.	• The candidate cannot cope with more than 1 or 2 basic verbs, frequently *had* and *was*. • The candidate displays almost no knowledge of past tenses of verbs. • Verbs used more than once may be written differently on each occasion. • The candidate has a very limited vocabulary. • Several English or "made-up" words may appear in the writing. • There are examples of serious dictionary misuse.
Very Poor	0	• The content is very basic OR • The candidate has not completed at least three of the core bullet points.	• (Virtually) nothing is correct. • Most of the errors are serious. • Very little is intelligible to a sympathetic native speaker.	• The candidate copes only with "have" and "am". • Very few words are correctly written in the foreign language. • English words are used. • There may be several examples of mother tongue interference. • There may be several examples of serious dictionary misuse.

Higher German
Listening/Writing
2008

SECTION A

1. *Any three from:*
   - (much) more freedom/freer/more free/more independent
   - can party/celebrate/stay out (with friends) until 3.00 am/the early morning/early in the morning
     can come in at 3.00 am/early in the morning
   - nobody can moan/complain about this/it
   - can have a long lie/stay in bed late/lie in/sleep as long as you want
     can wake/get up when you want
     do not have to get up early
   - can (go and) see/look at what(ever) you want

2. • birthday money from relatives
     OR
     saved her birthday money
   • half the money came from parents

3. • (book) flights/flight reservation/plane tickets/plane from Hamburg/plane to Glasgow
   • (book/reserve) bus (tickets) to airport
   • (sort out their) accommodation/youth hostel/somewhere to stay (in Scotland)/place to stay

4. • plane/flight delayed one hour/had to wait an hour for plane to leave
     plane/flight delayed because of fog/(bad) mist/weather
   • one friend/one of the group lost (his) wallet/purse

5. their room/the room for 5/the room they had booked not available/not free/double-booked
   OR
   they had to find another (youth-)hostel

6. *Any two from:*
   - big/large billiards/snooker/pool room/hall
   - lots of/many/full of games and books
   - barbecue/BBQ in garden
     OR
     small garden

7. so many shops
   OR
   lot(s) of/many shops in town/city centre

8. looked at/around/visited/went to see the castle
   OR
   strolled/wandered/meandered along Princes Street
   walked along/up/down Princes Street

9. *Any two from:*
   - rich/strong/wonderful/great culture
     a place of culture/very cultural/lots of culture
   - exciting/good/wicked/buzzing/healthy night-life
   - (very/really) good shopping/shops/shopping
   - possibilities/shopping facilities
     lots of good shops
   - wonderful/beautiful/spectacular/great countryside/nature/scenery/landscape
   - lakes/lochs/Highlands worth seeing

10. • went to Inverness (when she was) in Year 7
    • school/student exchange
       one year Scots go to Hamburg and the next year Germans go to Inverness

11. *Any one from:*
    - get to know/meet new people
    - get to know/meet/discover/experience/learn about/see
      a different/an exciting/another culture/way of life
    - it was great/really/good/lots of fun

Section B

Category	Mark	Content	Accuracy	Language Resource - Variety, Range, Structures
Very Good	10	• The topic is covered fully, in a balanced way, including a number of complex sentences. • Some candidates may also provide additional information. • A wide range of verbs/verb forms and constructions is used. There may also be a variety of tenses. • Overall this comes over as a competent, well thought-out response to the task which reads naturally	• The candidate handles all aspects of grammar and spelling accurately, although the language may contain some minor errors or even one more serious error. • Where the candidate attempts to use language more appropriate to post-Higher, a slightly higher number of inaccuracies need not detract from the overall very good impression.	• The candidate is comfortable with almost all the grammar used and generally uses a different verb or verb form in each sentence. • There is good use of a variety of tenses, adjectives, adverbs and prepositional phrases and, where appropriate, word order. • The candidate uses co-ordinating conjunctions and subordinate clauses throughout the writing. • The language flows well.
Good	8	• The topic is addressed, generally quite fully, and some complex sentences may be included. • The candidate uses a reasonable range of verbs/verb forms and other constructions.	• The candidate generally handles verbs and other parts of speech accurately but simply. • There may be some errors in spelling, adjective endings and, where relevant, case endings. • Use of accents may be less secure. • Where the candidate is attempting to use more complex vocabulary and structures, these may be less successful, although basic structures are used accurately. • There may be minor misuse of dictionary.	• There may be less variety in the verbs used. • Most of the complex sentences use co-ordinating conjunctions, and there may also be examples of subordinating conjunctions where appropriate. • At times the language may be more basic than might otherwise be expected at this level. • Overall the writing will be competent, mainly correct, but pedestrian.
Satisfactory	6	• The candidate uses mainly simple, more basic sentences. • The language is perhaps repetitive and uses a limited range of verbs and fixed phrases not appropriate to this level. • The topic may not be fully addressed. • In some cases, the content may be similar to that of good or very good examples, but with some serious accuracy issues.	• The verbs are generally correct, but basic. • Tenses may be inconsistent. • There are quite a few errors in other parts of speech – personal pronouns, gender of nouns, adjective endings, cases, singular/plural confusion – and in the use of accents. • Some prepositions may be inaccurate or omitted e.g. I go the town. • While the language may be reasonably accurate at times, the language structure may deteriorate significantly in places. • Overall, there is more correct than incorrect and there is the impression overall that the candidate can handle tenses.	• The candidate copes with the present tense of most verbs. • A limited range of verbs is used. • Candidate relies on a limited range of vocabulary and structures. • Where the candidate attempts constructions with modal verbs, these are not always successful. • Sentences may be basic and mainly brief. • There is minimal use of adjectives, probably mainly after "is" e.g. My friend is reliable. • The candidate has a weak knowledge of plurals. • There may be several spelling errors e.g. reversal of vowel combinations.

Section B (cont.)

Category	Mark	Content	Accuracy	Language Resource - Variety, Range, Structures
Unsatisfactory	4	• In some cases the content may be basic. • In other cases there may be little difference in content between Satisfactory and Unsatisfactory • The language is repetitive, with undue reliance on fixed phrases and a limited range of common basic verbs such as *to be, to have, to play, to watch*. • While the language used to address the more predictable aspects of the task may be accurate, serious errors occur when the candidate attempts to address a less predictable aspect. • The Personal Response may be presented as a single paragraph.	• Ability to form tenses is inconsistent. • In the use of the perfect tense the auxiliary verb is omitted on a number of occasions. • There may be confusion between the singular and plural form of verbs. • There are errors in many other parts of speech – gender of nouns, cases, singular/plural confusion – and in spelling and, where appropriate, word order. • Several errors are serious, perhaps showing mother tongue interference. • There may be one sentence which is not intelligible to a sympathetic native speaker. • Overall, there is more incorrect than correct.	• The candidate copes mainly only with predictable language. • There is inconsistency in the use of various expressions, especially verbs. • Sentences are more basic. • An English word may appear in the writing or a word may be omitted. • There may be an example of serious dictionary misuse.
Poor	2	• The content and language may be very basic. • However, in many cases the content may be little different from that expected at Unsatisfactory or even at Satisfactory.	• Many of the verbs are incorrect or even omitted. • There are many errors in other parts of speech – personal pronouns, gender of nouns, adjective endings, cases, singular/plural confusion – and in spelling and word order. • Prepositions are not used correctly. • The language is probably inaccurate throughout the writing. • Some sentences may not be understood by a sympathetic native speaker.	• The candidate cannot cope with more than 1 or 2 basic verbs, frequently "has" and "is". • Verbs used more than once may be written differently on each occasion. • The candidate has a very limited vocabulary. • Several English or "made-up" words may appear in the writing. • There are examples of serious dictionary misuse.
Very Poor	0	• The content is very basic.	• (Virtually) nothing is correct. • Most of the errors are serious. • Very little is intelligible to a sympathetic native speaker.	• The candidate copes only with "have" and "am". • Very few words are correctly written in the foreign language. • English words are used. • There may be several examples of mother tongue interference. • There may be several examples of serious dictionary misuse.

X060/301

NATIONAL QUALIFICATIONS 2005	FRIDAY, 27 MAY 9.00 AM – 10.40 AM	GERMAN HIGHER Reading and Directed Writing

45 marks are allocated to this paper. The value attached to each question is shown in the margin after each question.

You should spend approximately one hour on Section I and 40 minutes on Section II.

You may use a German dictionary.

SCOTTISH
QUALIFICATIONS
AUTHORITY

Read this magazine article carefully then answer **in English** the questions which follow it.

This article deals with a girl who has become a shopaholic.

Maria, 18: „Ich bin shopping-süchtig!"

Durch die Einkaufsstraßen schlendern, Klamotten anprobieren, sich etwas Cooles kaufen—für die meisten Teenager ist das einfach nur Freizeit-Fun. Doch für Maria
5 ist es viel mehr: Beim Shoppen fühlt sie sich wie ein Star, für den ein roter Teppich ausgerollt wird. Ihre Augen beginnen unnatürlich zu glänzen, ihr Herz schlägt schneller, sie hat Schmetterlinge im
10 Bauch—und will nur noch eins: kaufen!

„Es ist wie ein Anfall", erzählt Maria. „Immer das Gleiche: Ich sehe Popsängerinnen im TV—und sofort will ich auch so coole Klamotten haben wie sie!" So
15 will Maria auch aussehen—und der einzige Weg dorthin führt für sie durch die Shops der Einkaufszentren: „Eine Stimme in meinem Kopf sagt „Kauf dir das!" Und dann kann ich nicht anders. Ich will auch
20 schön sein, attraktiv und beliebt!"

Mit 13 Jahren war es noch ganz harmlos: Maria ging mit Freundinnen shoppen—wie Tausende anderer Girls. „Aber dann fingen die anderen an, über mich zu lästern und
25 Witze zu machen, weil ich immer massenhaft Einkaufstüten nach Hause schleppte—viel mehr als sie!" Maria zieht sich von ihrer Clique zurück, sie wird einsam.

Maria kann mit 50 Euro Taschengeld ihre
30 Einkaufssucht nicht finanzieren. Aber sie findet andere Quellen: Sie bekommt von den Großeltern immer wieder etwas zugesteckt. „Ich hab mir auch oft was geliehen und es gab Krach, weil ich es nicht zurückgezahlt,
35 sondern immer mehr gekauft habe. Zu Weihnachten oder zum Geburtstag wünschte ich mir von der Familie Geld—und bekam es auch." Schließlich beginnt Maria sogar ihr Sparkonto zu plündern!

40 „Mit 17 Jahren verdiente ich zum ersten Mal selbst etwas, rund 400 Euro im Monat. Und jetzt ging es erst richtig los, denn je mehr ich hatte, desto mehr gab ich aus! Meine Eltern meinten, dass es gut ist, wenn

ihre Tochter lernt, mit Geld umzugehen und 45 mischten sich nicht ein."

Und dann entdeckte Maria das Internet! Aussuchen, bestellen—und irgendwann zahlen. „Manchmal hatte ich keine Ahnung mehr, wie viel Geld ich schon ausgegeben 50 hatte." Die Geldsorgen bedrücken Maria immer stärker. Sie verbringt schlaflose Nächte. „Ich sah mich mit hohen Schulden, ohne die Möglichkeit, ein ganz normales Leben zu führen. Aber trotzdem konnte ich 55 das Shopping einfach nicht aufgeben."

Maria macht zwar Versuche, von ihrer Kaufsucht loszukommen. „Ich verordnete mir selbst ein „Stadtverbot" oder ging los, ohne Geld mitzunehmen. Doch dann stand 60 ich vor den bunt dekorierten Schaufenstern und schrieb Listen mit all den Dingen, die ich mir kaufen würde, sobald ich wieder Geld dabei hätte!"

Aber das tolle Gefühl beim Einkaufen 65 dauert nicht lange; wie bei einer Drogensucht braucht Maria immer höhere Dosen, kauft immer mehr, immer schneller. Und dann sitzt sie zu Hause auf ihrem Bett und weiß: Nichts hat sie durch ihre Einkäufe 70 geändert, gar nichts! „Ich brach immer häufiger ganz plötzlich in Tränen aus, wurde nervös, fing an zu zittern und konnte mich schließlich kaum noch konzentrieren." Marias Eltern sind vollkommen ratlos. Ist 75 ihre Tochter vielleicht krank?

„Meine Eltern haben mir gesagt, ich sollte zum Arzt. Und das war das Beste, was mir passieren konnte! Der Arzt hat lange mit mir geredet. Zum ersten Mal habe ich ganz offen 80 von meiner Shoppingsucht gesprochen. Ich habe zugegeben, wie unglücklich ich war."

„Der Arzt hat für mich dann den Kontakt zu einem Therapeuten gemacht, der sich mit dem Problem Kaufsucht auskennt. Vor zwei 85 Wochen hatte ich schon meine erste Sitzung bei ihm. Ich habe auch schon ein paar Erfolge zu verbuchen: Ich leihe mir kein

Geld mehr von meinen Freunden und habe
90 ihnen schon fast alles zurückgezahlt. Aber
das ist nur ein Anfang. Es ist noch zu früh,
um etwas darüber zu sagen, wann ich in ein
Geschäft gehen werde, ohne die Regale leer
zu kaufen. Ich will es aber schaffen und
endlich ein ganz normales Leben führen." 95

QUESTIONS

Marks

1. What effect does shopping have on Maria? **2 points**

2. Read lines 11–20.

   Why does Maria feel a constant need to shop? **2 points**

3. Read lines 21–28.

   How did Maria's addiction affect her relationship with her friends? **1 point**

4. Now read lines 29–39.

   Maria's pocket money is not enough to pay for her addiction. How did she finance her shopping sprees before she got a job? **3 points**

5. Read lines 40–46.

   (*a*) What happened when she started to earn money for the first time? **1 point**

   (*b*) Why did her parents not interfere? **1 point**

6. Read lines 47–56.

   (*a*) What does Maria say, which shows that her spending was out of control? **1 point**

   (*b*) How did Maria's money worries affect her? **3 points**

7. Read lines 57–64.

   (*a*) How did Maria try to cure her addiction? **1 point**

   (*b*) What shows that this did not work? **1 point**

8. Read lines 65–76.

   Why did Maria's parents end up wondering if she might be ill? **2 points**

9. Read lines 83–95.

   What success has she had, since seeing a therapist? **2 points**

   (20 points)

   = 20 marks

10. Translate into English:

    „Meine Eltern haben mir gesagt . . . wie unglücklich ich war." (lines 77–82) **10**

    (30)

    [Turn over for SECTION II on *Page four*

SECTION II—DIRECTED WRITING

Marks

Recently you did work experience in a German-speaking country. You have to write a report for the languages department in your school/college.

You must include the following information and **you should try to add** other relevant details:

- how you travelled and what you did during the journey

- what the job was and what hours you worked

- how you got on with your co-workers and what you liked/disliked about them

- what you did in the evenings

- what the local area was like

- what you got out of the experience.

Your report should be 150 – 180 words in length.

Marks will be deducted for any area of information that is omitted. **(15)**

[END OF QUESTION PAPER]

X060/303

NATIONAL
QUALIFICATIONS
2005

FRIDAY, 27 MAY
11.00 AM – 12.00 NOON

GERMAN
HIGHER
Listening Transcript

This paper must not be seen by any candidate.

The material overleaf is provided for use in an emergency only (eg the recording or equipment proving faulty) or where permission has been given in advance by SQA for the material to be read to candidates with special needs. The material must be read exactly as printed.

SCOTTISH
QUALIFICATIONS
AUTHORITY

Instructions to reader(s):

The dialogue below should be read in approximately 4 minutes. On completion of the first reading, pause for two minutes, then read the dialogue a second time.

Where special arrangements have been agreed in advance to allow the reading of the material, those sections marked **(m)** should be read by a male speaker and those marked **(f)** by a female.

Daniel, a 16-year-old German boy, is interviewed about his sporting activities and how they might clash with his love life.

(f) **Was machst du im Sportbereich?**

(m) Ich bin Torwart in einer Hockeymannschaft und zweimal pro Woche gehe ich zum Training. Wir haben auch ein- oder zweimal die Woche ein Spiel und jedes zweite Wochenende gibt es auch ein Auswärtsspiel irgendwoanders im Land, und das nimmt viel Zeit in Anspruch.

(f) **Gibt es dann Probleme mit deiner Freundin, weil du so viel Sport treibst?**

(m) Ja. Ich habe zwar keine Freundin, aber ich würde meine Mannschaft für kein Mädchen im Stich lassen. Sport ist mir sehr wichtig.

(f) **Was meinst du, kommt ein sportlicher Junge bei Mädchen besser an?**

(m) Hmm. Ich glaube, ja. Mädchen achten sehr auf das Aussehen von Jungs und finden es gut, wenn ein Junge eine sportliche Figur hat. Viele sagen zwar, Äußerlichkeiten seien nicht wichtig, aber ein dicker Freund ist vielen Mädchen dann doch peinlich.

(f) **Interessierst du dich auch außerhalb des Trainings für Sport?**

(m) Klar. Im Fernsehen gucke ich mir Sportsendungen an. Meine Lieblingssendung, „ran", sehe ich jeden Samstag. Ich lese auch regelmäßig Sportzeitschriften und, wenn ich Zeit habe, spiele ich mit meinem Bruder Tischtennis.

(f) **Wenn du so viel Zeit für Sport aufbringst—wo und wann willst du dann ein Mädchen kennen lernen?**

(m) Hmm. Das ist in der Tat nicht so einfach. Da ich jetzt 16 bin, hoffe ich, dass ich abends öfter weggehen darf. Ich denke, dass man beim Tanzen oder im Eiscafé gut Mädchen kennen lernen kann.

(f) **Angenommen, du bist frisch verliebt und du musst zwischen Freundin und Training entscheiden. Was würdest du machen?**

(m) Ah. Es würde mir schon schwer fallen, aber ich denke, Training und Turnier gehen vor. Ich bin der einzige Torwart und deshalb für die Mannschaft verantwortlich. Und eigentlich erwarte ich von meiner Freundin, dass sie das versteht.

(f) **Wärst du denn überhaupt bereit, dein Training wegen eines Mädchens einzuschränken?**

(m) Ich wäre zu einem Kompromiss bereit: Alle zwei Wochen lasse ich einmal das Training ausfallen. Das gilt aber nur, wenn die Freundin ihr Hobby auch einschränkt. Beide müssen etwas aufgeben.

(f) **Muss ein Mädchen sportlich sein, damit sie dich interessiert?**

(m) Nicht unbedingt, aber ein Pluspunkt wäre es schon. Vielleicht würde sie mich dann eher verstehen, wenn ich am Wochenende mal keine Zeit habe. Toll wäre es, wenn sie sich ab und zu ein Spiel unserer Mannschaft anschauen würde.

(f)   **Wie oft würdest du denn deine Freundin überhaupt sehen wollen?**

(m)   Nicht mehr als zweimal in der Woche—und natürlich am Samstagabend.

(f)   **Nicht öfter?**

(m)   Nein. Viele Pärchen in meinem Freundeskreis treffen sich täglich. Das finde ich nicht okay. Sie vergessen alles um sich herum. Meiner Meinung nach sollte man nicht die Freunde und die Mannschaft wegen einer Beziehung im Stich lassen.

[*END OF TRANSCRIPT*]

[BLANK PAGE]

FOR OFFICIAL USE

Examiner's Marks	
A	
B	

Total Mark

X060/302

NATIONAL
QUALIFICATIONS
2005

FRIDAY, 27 MAY
11.00 AM – 12.00 NOON

GERMAN
HIGHER
Listening/Writing

Fill in these boxes and read what is printed below.

Full name of centre

Town

Forename(s)

Surname

Date of birth

Day Month Year   Scottish candidate number   Number of seat

Do not open this paper until told to do so.

Answer Section A **in English** and Section B **in German**.

Section A

Listen carefully to the recording with a view to answering, **in English**, the questions printed in this answer book. Write your answers **clearly** and **legibly** in the spaces provided after each question.

You will have 2 minutes to study the questions before hearing the recording.

The recording will be played **twice**, with an interval of 2 minutes between the two playings.

You may make notes at any time but only in this answer book. **Draw your pen through any notes before you hand in the book.**

Move on to Section B when you have completed Section A: you will **not** be told when to do this.

Section B

Do not write your response in this book: **use the 4 page lined answer sheet**.

You will be told to insert the answer sheet inside this book before handing in your work.

You may consult a German dictionary at any time during **both** sections.

Before leaving the examination room you must give this book to the invigilator. If you do not, you may lose all the marks for this paper.

SCOTTISH
QUALIFICATIONS
AUTHORITY

Section A

Marks

Daniel, a 16-year-old German boy, is interviewed about his sporting activities and how they might clash with his love life.

1. (*a*) What demands does hockey make on Daniel's time each week?

    2 points

    (*b*) How often does he have a match somewhere else in the region?

    1 point

2. Why does Daniel think that boys who are into sport find it easier to attract a girlfriend?

    2 points

3. What interest does Daniel take in sport, apart from his hockey?

    2 points

4. (*a*) What is going to change, now that he is 16?

    1 point

    (*b*) Where does he think he might find a girlfriend?

    1 point

5. If Daniel had to choose between going to training and going out with his girlfriend, why would he go to training?

    1 point

DO NOT WRITE IN THIS MARGIN

Marks

6. (*a*) What compromise would Daniel be prepared to make, if he had a girlfriend?

2 points

(*b*) What would he expect the girl to do in return?

1 point

7. Why does Daniel think that having a girlfriend who is interested in sport might be a good thing?

2 points

8. When would Daniel want to see his girlfriend?

2 points

9. (*a*) How often do some of the couples he knows see each other?

1 point

(*b*) Why does he not approve of this?

2 points

(20 points)

= 20 marks

[Turn over for Section B on *Page four*

Marks

Section B

Für Daniel ist Sport sehr wichtig. Was ist für dich sehr wichtig? Musst du zwischen Freund/Freundin und anderen Interessen entscheiden? Wie kommst du denn zurecht?

Schreibe 120 – 150 Worte zu diesen Fragen!

10

(30)

USE THE 4 PAGE LINED ANSWER SHEET FOR YOUR ANSWER TO SECTION B

[END OF QUESTION PAPER]

[BLANK PAGE]

X060/301

NATIONAL
QUALIFICATIONS
2006

WEDNESDAY, 24 MAY
9.00 AM – 10.40 AM

GERMAN
HIGHER
Reading and
Directed Writing

45 marks are allocated to this paper. The value attached to each question is shown after each question.

You should spend approximately one hour on Section I and 40 minutes on Section II.

You may use a German dictionary.

SCOTTISH
QUALIFICATIONS
AUTHORITY

Read this magazine article carefully then answer **in English** the questions which follow it.

This article deals with school students in Hersbruck (Bavaria) who have part-time jobs.

Für Handy, Klamotten, Kino, Urlaub

Schüler bessern sich durch Jobs ihr Taschengeld auf—Die Schulleistung darf nicht darunter leiden.

Handy, Klamotten, Kino und Urlaub—das Leben eines Schülers kann ganz schön teuer werden. Dafür reicht das Taschengeld meist nicht aus, das wissen viele Jugendliche aus
5 leidvoller Erfahrung. Ferienjobs sind für sie deshalb eine willkommene Alternative zum elterlichen Geldbeutel. Mittlerweile gibt es aber zahlreiche Schüler, die nicht nur in den Ferien, sondern regelmäßig neben der
10 Schule arbeiten, um ihr eigenes Geld zu verdienen.

Einer von ihnen ist Sebastian Herbst. Zweimal pro Woche schwingt er sich in den Fahrradsattel, um Fernsehzeitschriften und
15 Illustrierte auszutragen. Seit zwei Jahren verschafft sich der 17-Jährige, der in die zehnte Klasse des Paul-Pfinzing-Gymnasiums geht, damit ein Stück finanzieller Unabhängigkeit von seinen
20 Eltern.

Das verdiente Geld gibt er hauptsächlich für Handy und Klamotten aus. Auch den Schüleraustausch nach Frankreich und die diesjährige Reise nach Schottland will er
25 damit bezahlen. Dass er den Job überhaupt bekommen hat, hat Sebastian eigentlich seiner Mutter zu verdanken, die damals in der Zeitung die Stellenanzeige las.

Die Arbeit selbst ist für ihn mittlerweile
30 zur reinen Routine geworden. So hat er sich den Bezirk, für den er zuständig ist, in drei Touren eingeteilt, die er dann nacheinander mit dem Fahrrad abfährt. Bei jedem Wetter natürlich, denn die Kunden wollen ihre
35 abonnierten Zeitschriften ja auch rechtzeitig erhalten. „Man muss sich an die Zeiten und Termine halten", sagt Sebastian. „Aber wenn es heiß ist oder wenn Glatteis ist, ist es schon blöd", gesteht er lächelnd: „Der Job
40 macht mir viel Spaß; es ist immerhin leicht verdientes Geld und meine Schularbeit leidet ja auch nicht darunter."

Finanzielle Unabhängigkeit war auch das Ziel von Susanne Hupfer. Früher jobbte sie gelegentlich als Babysitterin, seit längerem
45 bedient die 17-jährige Realschülerin nun aber schon im Café Corretto. Im Laden sah sie vor zwei Jahren das Stellengesuch aushängen, bewarb sich und nach einem Probearbeitstag hatte sie den Job. „Ein
50 Grund, warum ich unbedingt kellnern wollte, ist, weil zu dem Stundenlohn auch noch das Trinkgeld dazukommt", erklärt sie. „Zudem ist die Arbeit äußerst abwechslungsreich, denn jeder Gast ist
55 schließlich anders. Der Umgang mit den Menschen fällt mir aber leicht. Man lernt schnell, locker auf die Leute zuzugehen und auch unfreundlichen Gästen gegenüber freundlich zu sein. Aber es gibt Tage, da ist
60 es schon stressig."

Wegen der Abschlussprüfungen an der Realschule musste Susanne weniger Stunden machen, damit die Arbeit als Kellnerin ihre Schulnoten nicht beeinträchtigt. In der Tat
65 findet sie das Gegenteil: „In Kopfrechnen bin ich echt besser geworden", sagt sie lachend.

Auch Andreas Förthner arbeitet seit über zwei Jahren in direktem Kundenkontakt. In
70 einem Supermarkt räumt er zweimal pro Woche die Regale ein oder ist in der Getränkeabteilung für [1]das Leergut zuständig. Seine Eltern finden es schon gut, dass sich der 18-jährige Gymnasiast sein
75 eigenes Geld verdient. „Sein Bruder hat diesen Job früher immerhin auch einmal gemacht und mit der Schule hat es bislang auch keine Probleme gegeben", sagen sie.

„Ich weiß genau, wo man alles im
80 Supermarkt finden kann und welche Flaschen wir zurücknehmen dürfen", sagt Andreas. Wenn Kunden genervt und unfreundlich sind, hat er seine eigene Taktik entwickelt: „Man muss sympathisch sein und
85 den Kunden helfen."

Die Arbeit macht ihm Spaß und er verdient ja gut damit, aber vor allem ist sich Andreas über eines im Klaren: „Es ist eine gute 90 Erfahrung. Man bekommt ein anderes Gefühl fürs Geld und überlegt sich, wofür man es ausgibt; aber lebenslang möchte ich das auch nicht machen."

[1]**das Leergut = the empties**

QUESTIONS

Marks

1. Why do many young people find that they need a part-time job? — **2 points**

2. Sebastian Herbst is one of these students.

   (*a*) What exactly does he do? — **1 point**

   (*b*) What **two** major expenses does he want to pay for? — **1 point**

   (*c*) How did he come by his job? — **1 point**

3. Read lines 29–42.

   (*a*) How does Sebastian organise his work? — **2 points**

   (*b*) What comment does he make about the weather? — **1 point**

   (*c*) What **two** things does Sebastian say about his job? — **1 point**

Now read lines 43–61.

4. (*a*) What motivated Susanne Hupfer to find work? — **1 point**

   (*b*) Why did she particularly want to be a waitress? — **1 point**

5. What does Susanne say about dealing with people? — **2 points**

6. Read lines 62–68.

   (*a*) Why is Susanne working fewer hours just now? — **1 point**

   (*b*) In what way has her job helped her at school? — **1 point**

7. Read lines 69–79.

   (*a*) What does Andreas' job involve? — **2 points**

   (*b*) Why do his parents have no objections to his working? — **2 points**

8. Read lines 87–93.

   Why does Andreas feel his job has been a good experience? — **1 point**

9. Translate into English: — **(20 points)**

   = 20 marks

   „Ich weiß genau, . . . den Kunden helfen." (lines 80–86) — **10**

   (30)

[Turn over for SECTION II on *Page four*

SECTION II—DIRECTED WRITING

Marks

You recently took part in an exchange visit to Germany. One day your host family took you on a trip to a town some distance away.

On your return to Scotland, you send in an article **in German** for the newspaper of your exchange partner's school.

You must include the following information and **you should try to add** other relevant details:

- who all were in your host family and what their home was like

- what the family's local area was like and what there was to do there

- how the family spent a typical day

- what you did on the day you went on this special trip

- what you all did for food that day

- whether you would recommend the experience of an exchange trip to someone else.

Your report should be 150 – 180 words in length.

Marks will be deducted for any area of information that is omitted. **(15)**

[END OF QUESTION PAPER]

X060/303

NATIONAL
QUALIFICATIONS
2006

WEDNESDAY, 24 MAY
11.00 AM – 12.00 NOON

GERMAN
HIGHER
Listening Transcript

This paper must not be seen by any candidate.

The material overleaf is provided for use in an emergency only (eg the recording or equipment proving faulty) or where permission has been given in advance by SQA for the material to be read to candidates with additional support needs. The material must be read exactly as printed.

SCOTTISH
QUALIFICATIONS
AUTHORITY

©

> **Instructions to reader(s):**
>
> The dialogue below should be read in approximately 3 minutes. On completion of the first reading, pause for two minutes, then read the dialogue a second time.
>
> Where special arrangements have been agreed in advance to allow the reading of the material, those sections marked **(m)** should be read by a male speaker and those marked **(f)** by a female.

Katherina, a 21 year-old German who is studying in Scotland, talks about issues concerning a healthy lifestyle.

(m) **Ist für dich die Gesundheit wichtig?**

(f) Ja, die Gesundheit ist für mich sehr wichtig. Ich denke, dass Jugendliche fit sein sollten, damit sie auch noch gesund bleiben, wenn sie älter sind.

(m) **Was machst du denn, um fit zu bleiben?**

(f) Ich gehe regelmäßig mit meiner Freundin zusammen joggen, nehme am Badminton-Unterricht teil und spiele zweimal die Woche Volleyball.

(m) **Und passt du auf, was du isst ?**

(f) Ja, ich denke schon. Ich würde jetzt nicht jeden Tag zu McDonalds gehen oder mich von Fastfood ernähren, sondern achte schon darauf, dass ich viel Salat und Gemüse esse.

(m) **Ist Fastfood denn bei euch in Deutschland genauso beliebt wie hier in Schottland?**

(f) Ich denke, in Deutschland gehen weniger Leute zu McDonalds oder Burger King, aber hier in Schottland habe ich festgestellt, dass ganz viele Familien mit jungen Kindern sich von Fastfood ernähren.

(m) **Und apropos gesundes Essen, haben deine Eltern in dieser Sache immer ein gutes Beispiel gegeben?**

(f) Meine Eltern haben immer sehr darauf geachtet, dass wir jeden Tag viel Obst und nicht zu viel Süßigkeiten gegessen haben.

(m) **Und wie oft trinkst du Alkohol?**

(f) Ich trinke manchmal am Wochenende. Ab und zu ein Bier, aber nicht sehr regelmäßig.

(m) **Und gibt es ein Alkoholproblem in Deutschland?**

(f) In den Großstädten gibt es sicherlich ein Problem mit Alkohol. Aber ich denke, nicht mehr oder weniger als hier in Schottland. Ich glaube, das ist ziemlich gleich.

In Deutschland können die Jugendlichen schon mit 16 Bier oder Wein trinken und diese Getränke auch legal im Laden oder in einer Kneipe kaufen.

(m) **Wie steht's denn mit dem Rauchen? Das passt doch nicht zu einem gesunden Leben, oder?**

(f) Nein, Rauchen ist natürlich sehr ungesund. Ich selber rauche nicht und habe nie geraucht. Viele Jugendliche rauchen aber, weil es cool ist; Gruppenzwang—dann raucht man eben zusammen mal eine Zigarette. Ich denke, das ist in allen Ländern gleich.

(m) **Gibt es Unterschiede zwischen Schottland und Deutschland bezüglich der Gesundheit?**

(f) Ja, es gibt große Unterschiede. Es ist mir aufgefallen, dass sehr viele Menschen in Schottland zu dick sind und Gesundheitsprobleme haben, auf Grund ihres Gewichts. Hier sehe ich auch kleine Kinder, die sehr dick sind und keinen Sport treiben können. In Deutschland ist das nicht der Fall, meiner Meinung nach.

(m)   **Woran liegt das?**

(f)   In deutschen Schulen essen die meisten Kinder in der Pause ein Butterbrot oder einen Apfel, und man darf in der Schule keine Süßigkeiten verkaufen. Hier in Schottland sehe ich in den Pausen ganz viele Kinder mit Chipstüten herumstehen. So was kommt in Deutschland nicht vor. Und fast jedes Kind treibt auch am Nachmittag Sport, denn bei uns gibt es viele Sportvereine für Jugendliche.

[END OF TRANSCRIPT]

[BLANK PAGE]

FOR OFFICIAL USE

Examiner's Marks	
A	
B	

Total Mark

X060/302

NATIONAL
QUALIFICATIONS
2006

WEDNESDAY, 24 MAY
11.00 AM – 12.00 NOON

GERMAN
HIGHER
Listening/Writing

Fill in these boxes and read what is printed below.

Full name of centre

Town

Forename(s)

Surname

Date of birth
Day Month Year   Scottish candidate number   Number of seat

Do not open this paper until told to do so.

Answer Section A **in English** and Section B **in German**.

Section A

Listen carefully to the recording with a view to answering, **in English**, the questions printed in this answer book. Write your answers **clearly** and **legibly** in the spaces provided after each question.

You will have 2 minutes to study the questions before hearing the recording.

The recording will be played **twice**, with an interval of 2 minutes between the two playings.

You may make notes at any time but only in this answer book. **Draw your pen through any notes before you hand in the book.**

Move on to Section B when you have completed Section A: you will **not** be told when to do this.

Section B

Do not write your response in this book: **use the 4 page lined answer sheet**.

You will be told to insert the answer sheet inside this book before handing in your work.

You may consult a German dictionary at any time during **both** sections.

Before leaving the examination room you must give this book to the invigilator. If you do not, you may lose all the marks for this paper.

SCOTTISH
QUALIFICATIONS
AUTHORITY

SA X060/302 6/4370

Section A

Marks

Katherina, a 21 year-old German who is studying in Scotland, talks about issues concerning a healthy lifestyle.

1. Why does Katherina think that young people should keep fit?

1 point

2. What does Katherina do to keep fit?

2 points

3. In what ways does Katherina watch what she eats?

2 points

4. What differences concerning fast food does Katherina notice between Germany and Scotland?

2 points

5. How did Katherina's parents make sure she ate healthily?

2 points

Marks

6. How often does she drink alcohol?

1 point

7. (*a*) To what extent does Katherina think there is an alcohol problem in Germany?

1 point

(*b*) What is the law in Germany with regard to alcohol and young people?

2 points

8. What does Katherina say about smoking?

2 points

9. What health issues has she noticed in Scotland?

2 points

10. Why does Katherina think that children in Germany are not as overweight as many in Scotland?

3 points

(20 points)

= 20 marks

[Turn over for Section B on *Page four*

Marks

Section B

Und du, ist für dich die Gesundheit wichtig? Passt du darauf auf, was du isst und trinkst? Was hältst du von Alkohol und Zigaretten?

Schreibe 120 – 150 Worte zu diesen Fragen!

10

(30)

USE THE 4 PAGE LINED ANSWER SHEET FOR YOUR ANSWER TO SECTION B

[END OF QUESTION PAPER]

[BLANK PAGE]

X060/301

NATIONAL
QUALIFICATIONS
2007

WEDNESDAY, 30 MAY
9.00 AM – 10.40 AM

GERMAN
HIGHER
Reading and
Directed Writing

45 marks are allocated to this paper. The value attached to each question is shown after each question.

You should spend approximately one hour on Section I and 40 minutes on Section II.

You may use a German dictionary.

SCOTTISH
QUALIFICATIONS
AUTHORITY

©

SECTION I—READING

Read this magazine article carefully then answer **in English** the questions which follow it.

This article is about Germans who are thinking about or are actually living in Australia.

Wie ist es wirklich, fern der Heimat zu leben?

Immer mehr Deutsche wollen nach Australien. Ulrich Blos, zum Beispiel, träumt seit sechs Jahren von Australien. „Ich habe hier in Deutschland eine gute
5 Arbeit", sagt er, aber seit er 2001 eine Weile auf einer australischen Farm gearbeitet hat, hat er diesen Traum. „Wir sind im Busch gewandert. Da war nur Wald, nur Natur, so weit das Auge reicht. Deutschland ist mir
10 jetzt zu eng. Es gibt zu viel Stress und Leistungsdruck. Ob und wann wir tatsächlich nach Australien gehen, weiß ich noch nicht. Vielleicht, wenn die Kinder erwachsen sind."

15 Marie Merkel ist Krankenschwester in *Berlin*. „Mit meinen Qualifikationen habe ich in Australien gute Chancen. Ich würde natürlich meine dreijährige Tochter mitnehmen. Mit vier Jahren könnte sie dort
20 in die Schule gehen." Eigentlich gibt es für sie nur eine Hürde: die hohen Kosten für die Visa und den beruflichen Qualifikations-Test. Insgesamt würde es wohl etwa 2000 australische Dollar kosten und so viel Geld
25 hat sie nicht.

Gerhard Scheller hat seinen deutschen Pass abgegeben und ist jetzt stolz darauf, australischer Staatsbürger zu sein. Gerhard und seine Frau Britta haben sich kennen
30 gelernt, als sie in *Hamburg* Informatik studierten. Seit 1994 leben sie in einem Vorort von *Sydney*. Zurückkehren wollen sie nicht: Er begann in Australien mit einem eigenen Betrieb, seit sieben Jahren fährt er
35 Trucks. Sein Fotoalbum erzählt eine Geschichte vom selbst ausgebauten Haus mit Garten, von schönen Tagen am Meer und Festen mit Freunden. „Der Anfang kann einsam sein, wenn man stumm in der Ecke
40 sitzt und nicht einmal Witze auf Englisch verstehen kann", sagt Gerhard. „Und um mit Australiern reden zu können, muss man etwas über Politik, Sport und Humor in Australien wissen."

45 „Und noch etwas sollten künftige Auswanderer bedenken", sagt Gerhard: „Es kostet sehr viel Geld und Zeit, wieder nach Deutschland zu kommen. Wir waren erst nach acht Jahren das erste Mal in der Lage, für vier Wochen nach Deutschland zu 50 fliegen." Gerhards Fotos erzählen auch von der harten Arbeit hinter dem australischen Traum. Oft arbeitet er sechs Tage die Woche. „Ich habe noch nie in meinem Leben so lange und so hart gearbeitet. Keine 55 Mittagspause trotz 40 Grad im Schatten—die Leute hier arbeiten einfach weiter. Der Lohn ist geringer als in Deutschland und die Lebenshaltungskosten in *Sydney* viel höher." Was vermisst er an 60 Deutschland? Gerhard lacht. „Currywurst. Die bekomme ich hier nirgendwo." Heimweh kann auch die Form einer Wurst annehmen.

Für Antje Eildermann ist Australien ein 65 Geruch und ein Lachen. „Es riecht hier oft wochenlang nach Rauch", sagt Antje, die vor zwei Jahren von *Berlin* nach *Sydney* gezogen ist. Der Rauch kommt ab August von den Waldbränden in den Blue Mountains. Das 70 Lachen stammt von einem Vogel. Es ist der Ruf des Kookaburra, eines australischen Vogels, der hier überall vorkommt. Eigentlich wollte Antje gar nicht auswandern, sondern kam nach dem 75 Studium zum Praktikum. „Dann habe ich Marcel getroffen, geheiratet und bin geblieben." Manchmal vermisst sie Deutschland—„nicht das Land, eher den Alltag, den [1]Tchibo um die Ecke oder so, 80 aber ich liebe *Sydney*. Die Menschen sind sehr offen, man knüpft schnell Kontakte."

„Das Schulsystem finde ich aber nicht so gut," sagt Antje. „Gute Schulen sind in Australien in der Regel privat und relativ 85 teuer." Noch haben die beiden keine Kinder, „aber wenn wir Kinder bekommen, sollten sie eher in Deutschland zu Schule gehen", sagt sie. Es gibt diesen Plan, nach *Berlin* zurückzuziehen. „Mein Mann würde 90 mitkommen, er liebt Deutschland und war schon oft da", sagt sie. Sie möchte auch aus beruflichen Gründen zurückkehren. Ihre Eltern haben eine Firma in *Berlin*, die Antje 95 eines Tages übernehmen möchte. „In drei bis fünf Jahren," sagt Antje, „werden wir nach Deutschland auswandern." Vielleicht wird sie dann eines Tages, auf dem Weg zum

[1]Tchibo, einen eingebildeten Feuergeruch wahrnehmen und ein Lachen vermissen. 100 Heimweh ist ein vielseitiges Gefühl.

[1]**Tchibo = a shop selling a brand of German coffee**

QUESTIONS

Marks

1. (*a*) What experience made Ulrich Blos start dreaming about a life in Australia? **1 point**

   (*b*) How does he feel about Germany now? **2 points**

   (*c*) When might he go to Australia to live? **1 point**

2. Read lines 15–25.

   (*a*) Why is Marie Merkel thinking about moving to Australia? **2 points**

   (*b*) What is the only thing that is stopping her from going? **1 point**

3. Read lines 26–44.

   What does Gerhard Scheller say about starting a new life in Australia? **2 points**

4. Now read lines 45–64.

   (*a*) What do Germans thinking of emigrating to Australia need to be aware of, according to Gerhard? **1 point**

   (*b*) What information does Gerhard give about his working life? Mention **three** things. **3 points**

5. Read lines 65–82.

   (*a*) What sums up Australia as far as Antje Eildermann is concerned? **2 points**

   (*b*) Antje never intended to emigrate. Why did she stay in Australia? **1 point**

   (*c*) What does she like about people in Sydney? **1 point**

6. Read lines 83–101.

   (*a*) What does Antje say about schools in Australia? **1 point**

   (*b*) Why will they probably return to Berlin one day? **2 points**

   (20 points)

   = 20 marks

7. Translate into English:

   „Gerhard Scheller hat . . . Vorort von *Sydney*." (lines 26–32) **10**

   (30)

   [Turn over for SECTION II on *Page four*

SECTION II—DIRECTED WRITING

Marks

You have travelled to Germany to spend a holiday with German friends of your parents. While you are there, you are asked to baby-sit one day from 3.00 pm until 8.00 pm.

When you return to Scotland, you have to write a report **in German** for the Languages department in your school/college.

You must include the following information and **you should try to add** other relevant details:

* what the journey to Germany was like and how you felt travelling on your own

* who all was in the family and what they were like

* where the family house was situated and what it was like

* how you spent the five hours with the children while their parents were out

* what you did usually on your other evenings while in Germany

* why you would/would not baby-sit for this German family again.

Your report should be 150 – 180 words in length.

Marks will be deducted for any area of information that is omitted.   (15)

[END OF QUESTION PAPER]

X060/303

NATIONAL
QUALIFICATIONS
2007

WEDNESDAY, 30 MAY
11.00 AM – 12.00 NOON

GERMAN
HIGHER
Listening Transcript

This paper must not be seen by any candidate.

The material overleaf is provided for use in an emergency only (eg the recording or equipment proving faulty) or where permission has been given in advance by SQA for the material to be read to candidates with additional support needs. The material must be read exactly as printed.

SCOTTISH
QUALIFICATIONS
AUTHORITY

Instructions to reader(s):

The dialogue below should be read in approximately 4 minutes. On completion of the first reading, pause for two minutes, then read the dialogue a second time.

Where special arrangements have been agreed in advance to allow the reading of the material, those sections marked **(m)** should be read by a male speaker and those marked **(f)** by a female.

Candidates have two minutes to study the questions before the transcript is read.

Nicole, a German-language assistant, is interviewed about her Abitur and what she did after the exams.

(m) Nicole, du hast letztes Jahr Abitur gemacht. Wie war diese Zeit für dich?

(f) Ja, ich habe letzten Mai Abitur gemacht. Das war eine sehr stressige Zeit. Wir hatten wahnsinnig viel zu tun. Es gab viel zu lernen, viele Bücher zu lesen und Aufsätze zu schreiben. Ich hatte damals sehr viel Stress; ich erinnere mich noch ganz gut an alles.

(m) Wie hast du dich darauf vorbereitet—also auf das Abitur?

(f) Wir haben einen Lernplan gemacht, um den ganzen Stoff unterzubringen. Wir haben von Woche zu Woche verschiedene Sachen gelernt und das immer wiederholt. Ich hatte überhaupt keine Freizeit mehr. Ich konnte meine Freunde nicht mehr so oft treffen und hatte fast keine Zeit mehr, Sport zu machen. Und ja, die Zeit war einfach sehr knapp.

(m) Und wie ist das Abitur gelaufen?

(f) Es ist gut gelaufen. Ich war sehr zufrieden mit meinen Noten; ich hatte einen Durchschnitt von 1,5, was sehr gut ist.

(m) Was habt ihr nach dem vielen Stress gemacht, um zu feiern?

(f) Wir haben drei bis vier Tage nur Party gemacht. Außerdem hat die Schule eine große Feier organisiert—mit der ganzen Jahrgangsstufe.

(m) Und als Belohnung hast du was gemacht?

(f) Ja, dann sind wir in Urlaub auf die Insel Fuerteventura gefahren. Wir sind eine große Clique von ungefähr zehn Leuten und wir hatten diesen Urlaub schon länger geplant. Es gab viel zu planen—die Flüge, die Unterkunft und die ganzen Unternehmungen—und das war unsere Belohnung für das Abi.

(m) Wie habt ihr die Reise organisiert?

(f) Wir haben das per Internet gemacht und haben uns Informationen aus dem Reisebüro geholt.

(m) Lief alles nach Plan?

(f) Ja, eigentlich schon. Aber es sind drei Leute verhindert gewesen. Corinna konnte nicht mitgehen—wegen ihrer Eltern. Sie haben es ihr verboten. Mario konnte nicht mit; er hatte eine Arbeit gefunden. Und eine Freundin von mir—Nadine—wurde krank. So konnte auch sie nicht mitgehen. Aber ansonsten lief alles nach Plan.

(m) Und habt ihr Spaß auf der Insel gehabt?

(f) Ja, es war cool—super. Wir hatten viel Spaß. Wir sind viel weggegangen. Wir haben am Meer in der Sonne ausgespannt und wir haben eigentlich eine Woche gar nichts gemacht —ein paar Ausflüge am Tag, einige Sehenswürdigkeiten angeschaut—wirklich richtig locker und ohne Stress.

(m) **Ihr habt das Abitur richtig gefeiert, ja? Würdest du das weiterempfehlen?**

(f) Ja, ich würde es auf jeden Fall weiterempfehlen. Es war eine sehr, sehr schöne Zeit. Und die Erholung im Urlaub hat man sich dann richtig verdient. Es ist auch die letzte Gelegenheit, mit den Freunden so viel Zeit zu verbringen, bevor man auf die Uni geht oder eine Arbeit sucht. Und deshalb würde ich es weiterempfehlen, die Zeit einfach zu genießen und viel mit Freunden zu unternehmen.

[END OF TRANSCRIPT]

[BLANK PAGE]

FOR OFFICIAL USE

Examiner's Marks	
A	
B	

Total
Mark

X060/302

NATIONAL QUALIFICATIONS 2007	WEDNESDAY, 30 MAY 11.00 AM – 12.00 NOON	**GERMAN HIGHER** Listening/Writing

Fill in these boxes and read what is printed below.

Full name of centre

Town

Forename(s)

Surname

Date of birth

Day Month Year   Scottish candidate number   Number of seat

Do not open this paper until told to do so.

Answer Section A **in English** and Section B **in German**.

Section A

Listen carefully to the recording with a view to answering, **in English**, the questions printed in this answer book. Write your answers **clearly** and **legibly** in the spaces provided after each question.

You will have 2 minutes to study the questions before hearing the dialogue for the first time.

The dialogue will be played **twice**, with an interval of 2 minutes between the two playings.

You may make notes at any time but only in this answer book. **Draw your pen through any notes before you hand in the book.**

Move on to Section B when you have completed Section A: you will **not** be told when to do this.

Section B

Do not write your response in this book: **use the 4 page lined answer sheet**.

You will be told to insert the answer sheet inside this book before handing in your work.

You may consult a German dictionary at any time during **both** sections.

Before leaving the examination room you must give this book to the invigilator. If you do not, you may lose all the marks for this paper.

SCOTTISH
QUALIFICATIONS
AUTHORITY

©

Section A

Marks

Nicole, a German-language assistant, is interviewed about her Abitur and what she did after the exams.

1. What made Nicole's Abitur so stressful? **2 points**

2. (*a*) How did she prepare for the exams? **1 point**

    (*b*) How did this affect her free time? **2 points**

3. How did she do in her Abitur? **1 point**

4. What celebrations followed the exams? **2 points**

5. (*a*) Nicole's reward was a holiday on Fuertaventura. With whom did she go? **1 point**

    (*b*) What did they have to plan? **2 points**

Marks

5. **(continued)**

   (c) How did they go about organising their trip?   **1 point**

6. In what way did things not quite go according to plan?   **3 points**

7. How did they spend their time during the holiday?   **3 points**

8. Why would Nicole recommend doing something like this with friends?   **2 points**

**(20 points)
= 20 marks**

[Turn over for Section B on *Page four*

Marks

Section B

Und du, was hast du vor, diesen Sommer nach den Prüfungen zu machen? Fährst du mit den Eltern oder Freunden in Urlaub oder musst du einen Job finden?

Schreibe 120 – 150 Worte zu diesen Fragen!

10

(30)

USE THE 4 PAGE LINED ANSWER SHEET FOR YOUR ANSWER TO SECTION B

[END OF QUESTION PAPER]

[BLANK PAGE]

X060/301

NATIONAL
QUALIFICATIONS
2008

THURSDAY, 5 JUNE
9.00 AM – 10.40 AM

GERMAN
HIGHER
Reading and
Directed Writing

45 marks are allocated to this paper. The value attached to each question is shown after each question.

You should spend approximately one hour on Section I and 40 minutes on Section II.

You may use a German dictionary.

SECTION I—READING

Read this magazine article carefully then answer **in English** the questions which follow it.

This article is about a German girl, Sabrina Sadowski, who is spending a year in the United States as an au pair, living and working in a family.

Zwischen Abenteuer und Wahnsinn

Viele Jugendliche beenden ihre Schulzeit und fragen sich, was sie in Zukunft machen sollen. Studium oder Ausbildung?—wenn studieren, was studieren? Zu Hause bleiben
5 oder ausziehen?—wenn ausziehen, wohin denn? Und einige haben vielleicht gar keine Lust, sofort von der Schule an die Uni zu gehen. Wer würde sich da nicht noch ein Jahr Auszeit wünschen, um sich darüber klar
10 zu werden, was man genau will.

Vor einem Jahr ging es mir nicht anders. Deshalb war mir relativ schnell klar: Ich gehe als Au-pair in die Staaten! Es war die beste Entscheidung, die ich je gemacht habe.
15 Natürlich habe ich Horrorgeschichten über versklavte Au-pairs gehört, aber trotzdem stand ich irgendwann am Flughafen.

Das war vor elf Monaten. Ich habe in dieser Zeit wunderbare Menschen kennen
20 gelernt, zahlreiche neue Dinge erlebt und bin viel selbständiger geworden. Ich habe auch mein Englisch auf ein hohes Niveau bringen können.

Während des Au-pair-Jahres in den Staaten
25 muss man je nach Programm sechs bis zwölf „Credits" sammeln. Diese bekommt man durch einen Collegebesuch, Freiwilligenarbeit oder durch Sprachkurse. Ich zum Beispiel habe einen Erste-Hilfe- und einen
30 Spanischkursus abgeschlossen.

In meiner Familie bin ich für zwei Schulkinder verantwortlich. Daher habe ich jeden Morgen frei. Am Nachmittag bin ich hauptsächlich dazu da, die Kinder zur
35 richtigen Zeit an den richtigen Ort zu bringen und ihnen am Abend etwas zu kochen. Jedes Wochenende und jeden Abend habe ich frei. Unter der Woche treffe ich mich meistens mit Freunden in Cafés,
40 zum Videoabend oder in einer Karaokebar. Am Wochenende erkunden wir New York. Ich lebe mit meiner Gastfamilie in New Jersey. Nach einer knappen Stunde Zugfahrt stehe ich mitten auf dem Broadway in
45 Manhattan.

Aber die Geschichten von Horrorfamilien sind leider nicht alle falsch. So kann es passieren, dass ihr in eine Familie mit zwei hyperaktiven Kindern geratet oder dass eine unfreundliche, junge Leute hassende Oma 50 mit im Haus wohnt. Dass ihr jeden Abend bis 22 Uhr arbeiten müsst, oder dass ihr im Kühlschrank nur bestimmte Dinge essen dürft. Wenn ihr dann abends total fertig, unglücklich und müde in euer Bett fallt, 55 welches sich in einem winzigen Raum unter der Treppe befindet, dann werdet ihr euch doch fragen, wieso ihr dieses Leben mit eurem geliebten Zuhause getauscht habt.

Eine Freundin von mir arbeitet bei einer 60 Familie, wo die Eltern mit ihren Kindern so wenig wie möglich zu tun haben wollen. Jeden Morgen muss sie als erste Aufgabe dem achtjährigen Sohn 70 Tabletten geben und danach das Kind zum Psychiater fahren. 65 Laut dem Psychiater sind die Tabletten nichts als Vitamine!

Es ist fast unmöglich, die „perfekte" Familie zu finden. Hier und da muss man sich anpassen und Regeln akzeptieren. Viele 70 Au-pairs haben unter der Woche „Ausgangssperre". Manche müssen schon um 22 Uhr zu Hause sein. Andere können die ganze Nacht wegbleiben, solange sie am nächsten Morgen wieder da sind, um die 75 Kinder zu wecken.

Familien hier sind so unterschiedlich wie in Deutschland auch. Um die passende Familie zu finden, ist es sinnvoll, so ehrlich wie möglich zu sein und sich ganz genau zu 80 überlegen, was man von dem Jahr erwartet. Bei dem telefonischen Interview mit den Familien hat man die Chance, alle möglichen Fragen zu stellen. Man muss nicht unbedingt für Kinder schwärmen, aber 85 hassen sollte man sie auch nicht gerade.

Ich jedenfalls würde jedem ein solches Jahr empfehlen. Wenn man sich nach dem Motto „Was mich nicht umbringt, macht mich stärker!" in den Flieger setzt, kann kaum 90 etwas schief gehen, und man kann sich auf ein tolles Jahr freuen. Neue Erfahrungen sind zumindest garantiert—positive wie negative.

QUESTIONS

Marks

1. According to paragraph one, what questions might young people ask themselves at the end of their school career?

   2 points

2. Read lines 11–23.

   (*a*) How does Sabrina feel about her choice of going to America as an au pair?

   1 point

   (*b*) Eleven months on, what has been good about the experience?

   Mention **two** things.

   2 points

3. Read lines 24–30.

   (*a*) What can au pairs do to collect the credits required by their programmes?

   Mention **two** things.

   1 point

   (*b*) What has Sabrina chosen?

   1 point

4. Now read lines 31–45.

   (*a*) How does she spend her free time during the week?

   1 point

   (*b*) How is it easy for her to explore New York at the weekend?

   1 point

5. Read lines 46–59.

   (*a*) Some au pairs have unpleasant experiences. Give details of **three** of these.

   3 points

   (*b*) What unpleasant accommodation are some au pairs given?

   1 point

6. Read lines 60–67.

   (*a*) What does she say about the parents her friend worked for?

   1 point

   (*b*) What did her friend have to do each day?

   1 point

7. Read lines 68–76.

   Give details of some of the different rules which au pairs must accept.

   2 points

8. Read lines 77–86.

   What advice does the author give about finding a suitable family?

   1 point

9. Read lines 87–94.

   Why should the au pair adopt the motto "what doesn't kill me will make me stronger"?

   2 points

   (20 points)

   = 20 marks

10. Translate into English:

    „In meiner Familie . . . etwas zu kochen." (lines 31–37)

    10

    (30)

    [Turn over for SECTION II on *Page four*

SECTION II—DIRECTED WRITING

Marks

Last summer your parents arranged a house exchange with a German family.

On your return to Scotland, you are asked to write a report **in German** for the website through which the exchange was arranged.

You must include the following information and **you should try to add** other relevant details:

- how you travelled to the house in Germany **and** how you found the journey

- where exactly the house was situated **and** what it was like, compared with your own home

- what your daily routine was, while you were there

- what you did for food throughout your visit

- a family day-trip you went on, while you were in Germany

- whether your family would like to have another house-exchange and why/why not.

Your report should be 150 – 180 words in length.

Marks will be deducted for any area of information that is omitted. **(15)**

[END OF QUESTION PAPER]

X060/303

NATIONAL
QUALIFICATIONS
2008

THURSDAY, 5 JUNE
11.00 AM – 12.00 NOON

GERMAN
HIGHER
Listening Transcript

This paper must not be seen by any candidate.

The material overleaf is provided for use in an emergency only (eg the recording or equipment proving faulty) or where permission has been given in advance by SQA for the material to be read to candidates with additional support needs. The material must be read exactly as printed.

Instructions to reader(s):

The dialogue below should be read in approximately 5 minutes. On completion of the first reading, pause for two minutes, then read the dialogue a second time.

Where special arrangements have been agreed in advance to allow the reading of the material, those sections marked **(m)** should be read by a male speaker and those marked **(f)** by a female.

Candidates have two minutes to study the questions before the transcript is read.

Steffi, a 20 year-old German who is spending a year in Scotland, talks about earlier trips she has made here.

(m) **Hatten deine Eltern nichts dagegen, dass du ohne sie nach Schottland fliegst?**

(f) Ich bin schon einmal ohne meine Eltern weggefahren. Das hat wunderbar geklappt! Ich glaube, dass meine Eltern mir deshalb bei dieser Reise noch mehr vertrauen!

(m) **Was sind die Vorteile, wenn man ohne Eltern wegfährt?**

(f) Wenn ich ohne Eltern verreise, bin ich viel freier. Ich kann also mit meinen Freunden bis 3 Uhr morgens feiern gehen und niemand meckert darüber!

Wir konnten auch immer ausschlafen und dann einfach das anschauen, worauf wir Lust hatten.

(m) **Woher hast du das Geld für die Reise bekommen?**

(f) Ich kriege oft Geld von meinen Verwandten zu meinem Geburtstag. Davon habe ich etwas gespart. Aber ungefähr die Hälfte des Geldes habe ich von meinen Eltern bekommen.

(m) **Was musstest du vor der Abfahrt alles organisieren?**

(f) Wir mussten natürlich die Flüge buchen und dann noch den Bus zum Flughafen reservieren. Um die Unterkunft haben wir uns auch noch gekümmert. Wir haben uns eine schöne, zentral gelegene Jugendherberge ausgesucht und diese dann im Internet gebucht.

(m) **Wie bist du nach Schottland gereist?**

(f) Ich habe mich mit meinen Freunden am Hamburger Hauptbahnhof getroffen. Dann sind wir zusammen mit dem Bus zum Flughafen gefahren. Danach sind wir von Hamburg nach Glasgow geflogen.

(m) **Gab es irgendwelche Zwischenfälle, als ihr unterwegs wart?**

(f) Schon in Hamburg fing der Ärger an! Unser Flugzeug konnte aufgrund des dichten Nebels nicht pünktlich starten. Wir mussten circa eine Stunde warten! Einer meiner Freunde, Thomas, hat am Flughafen auch noch sein Portemonnaie verloren!

(m) **Hattet ihr Probleme mit der Unterkunft?**

(f) Wir hatten ja ein Zimmer für uns fünf gebucht. Aber als wir in unserer Jugendherberge ankamen, sagten sie uns, dass so ein Zimmer nicht mehr frei wäre. Wir haben jedoch ganz schnell eine neue, schöne Jugendherberge gefunden.

(m) **Gab es Freizeitmöglichkeiten in der Jugendherberge?**

(f) Es gab einen großen Billardraum und im Wohnzimmer gab es viele Spiele und Bücher, die man benutzen konnte. Im kleinen Garten stand sogar ein Grill. Wenn es nicht geregnet hat, haben wir einen gemütlichen Abend draußen verbracht.

(m) **Was hast du alles in Glasgow unternommen?**

(f) In Glasgow haben wir uns zum Beispiel die Kunstgalerie angesehen. Einkaufen waren wir natürlich auch, die Innenstadt hat ja so viele Geschäfte! Außerdem gibt es in Glasgow eine so große Auswahl an Klubs und Kneipen.

(m) **Warst du nur in Glasgow?**

(f) Nein, nach ein paar Tagen in Glasgow sind wir nach Edinburgh gefahren. Wir haben uns die bekannte Burg angeschaut und sind die Princes Street entlang geschlendert. Dann führte uns unsere Reise in den Norden. Es ging nach Fort William und dort sind wir wandern gegangen.

(m) **Würdest du Schottland als Reiseziel empfehlen?**

(f) Schottland ist auf jeden Fall eine Reise wert. Die Städte haben ein reiches Kulturangebot, ein aufregendes Nachtleben und sehr gute Einkaufsmöglichkeiten! Gleichzeitig kann man in Schottland eine wunderbare Natur erleben—die vielen Seen und das Hochland sind sehr sehenswert.

(m) **Warst du zum ersten Mal in Großbritannien?**

(f) Nein. In der 7. Klasse sind wir nach Inverness gereist. Unsere Schule in Hamburg und die in Inverness haben ein Austauschprogramm. In einem Jahr kommen die schottischen Schüler nach Hamburg und im nächsten Jahr fliegen die deutschen Jugendlichen nach Inverness. Das ist eine tolle Möglichkeit ein neues Land kennen zu lernen.

(m) **Würdest du eine Auslandserfahrung, wie diese Reise nach Schottland, anderen Jugendlichen weiter empfehlen?**

(f) Ich würde diesen Trip auf jeden Fall weiter empfehlen! Wir haben neue Menschen und eine andere, spannende Kultur kennen gelernt! Es hat uns allen richtig viel Spaß gemacht!

[END OF TRANSCRIPT]

[BLANK PAGE]

FOR OFFICIAL USE

Examiner's Marks	
A	
B	

Total Mark

X060/302

NATIONAL
QUALIFICATIONS
2008

THURSDAY, 5 JUNE
11.00 AM – 12.00 NOON

GERMAN
HIGHER
Listening/Writing

Fill in these boxes and read what is printed below.

Full name of centre

Town

Forename(s)

Surname

Date of birth

Day Month Year   Scottish candidate number   Number of seat

Do not open this paper until told to do so.

Answer Section A **in English** and Section B **in German**.

Section A

Listen carefully to the recording with a view to answering, **in English**, the questions printed in this answer book. Write your answers **clearly and legibly** in the spaces provided after each question.

You will have 2 minutes to study the questions before hearing the dialogue for the first time.

The dialogue will be played **twice**, with an interval of 2 minutes between the two playings.

You may make notes at any time but only in this answer book. **Draw your pen through any notes before you hand in the book.**

Move on to Section B when you have completed Section A: you will **not** be told when to do this.

Section B

Do not write your response in this book: **use the 4 page lined answer sheet**.

You will be told to insert the answer sheet inside this book before handing in your work.

You may consult a German dictionary at any time during **both** sections.

Before leaving the examination room you must give this book to the invigilator. If you do not, you may lose all the marks for this paper.

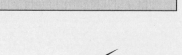

SA X060/302 6/6170

Section A

Marks

Steffi, a 20 year-old German who is spending a year in Scotland, talks about earlier trips she has made here.

1. What are the advantages of going on holiday without your parents? **3 points**

2. How **exactly** did she get the money for the holiday? **2 points**

3. What **three** things did they have to organise before leaving? **3 points**

4. What went wrong before they even left Hamburg? **2 points**

5. What difficulty did they have with their accommodation? **1 point**

Marks

6. What facilities did their accommodation have?　　**2 points**

7. Why did they enjoy shopping in Glasgow?　　**1 point**

8. What did they do in Edinburgh?　　**1 point**

9. What does she say about Scotland as a tourist destination?　Give **two** details.　　**2 points**

10. What information does she give about her first visit to Scotland?　　**2 points**

11. Why would Steffi recommend a trip abroad?　　**1 point**

(20 points)
= 20 marks

[Turn over for Section B on *Page four*

Marks

Section B

Und du, würdest du mit Freunden, mit der Familie oder alleine verreisen? Welche Art von Urlaub sagt dir zu—zum Beispiel Relaxen am Meer oder durch Europa reisen?

Schreibe 120 – 150 Worte zu diesen Fragen!

10

(30)

USE THE 4 PAGE LINED ANSWER SHEET FOR YOUR ANSWER TO SECTION B

[END OF QUESTION PAPER]

[BLANK PAGE]

[BLANK PAGE]

[BLANK PAGE]

[BLANK PAGE]

[BLANK PAGE]

Acknowledgements

Leckie and Leckie is grateful to the copyright holders, as credited, for permission to use their material:

The following companies have very generously given permission to reproduce their copyright material free of charge: Heinrich-Bauer Zeitschriften Verlag KG for the article 'Maria, 18 "Ich bin shopping-suchtig"', taken from Magazine: Bravo Girl No. 21, September 2003 (2005 Higher Paper pp 2-3).